AF437701

THE HEALING

OF

SOULS

IBN AL-JAWZI

Table of Contents

Preface

This is an abridged translation of Ibn Al-Jawzi's 'Tibb al-Ruhani'.

This book is full of wisdom and an excellent read. It will guide you to live a successful life in this world and the Hereafter. This book requires repeated readings to fully grasp the great wisdom and knowledge of Shaikh Ibn Al-Jawzi (Allah have mercy on him).

All that is righteous in this book comes from Allah alone, and all that is evil comes from the one who has abridged this book and Shaitaan.

CHAPTER 1: THE VIRTUE OF REASON

People have differed in the essence of reason and its place in the body. This explains the fact why this topic has been studied very extensively. Also, many hadiths have been reported that demonstrate the virtues and excellence of reason.

You can tell the excellence of a thing by its fruits. One of the fruits of reason and intellect is acquiring the knowledge of the Creator, the Exalted. This is because a person reasons and contemplates the signs of the existence of the Creator until they know Him. He examines the evidence of the truthfulness of the PROPHETs through reasoning (and through his mind) until he believes them (and recognizes their truthfulness).

Reason encourages obedience to ALLAH and His Messenger. Through reason, a person plans to achieve what is difficult to achieve. The mind helps to tame the animals. It teaches people to build ships that would help them achieve what the sea hid from them.

On the other hand, reason taught people to renounce the life of this world in favor of the hereafter. Humans have an advantage over animals because of their reason and intellect. By reasoning, humans are ready to receive, understand, and synthesize information and this distinguishes them from other living animals. This is what blessed a man to receive the speech of **ALLAH** and His commandments. In this way, man attains the highest ranks that his species can achieve for the benefit of this world and the hereafter, both in knowledge and in action.

A reasonable intellect always agrees with the guidance of the Qur'an and the Sunna. Reason prevents a person from doing what is inappropriate for a servant of **ALLAH**. By reasoning, a person can hold himself back from the vain desires of his heart. With the intellect, a person can see the merits and drawbacks of things and then act on that knowledge. A person is not considered wise if he does not act on useful knowledge.

Reason and intellect guide a person to distinguish between wisdom and stupidity. A person who does not act according to their reasoning and what they think is right is neither wise nor intelligent. We should therefore use our minds and intellects to follow the Quran and Sunnah and to heal our hearts.

CHAPTER 2: THE DISPRAISE OF DESIRES (AL-HAWA)

Al-Hawa refers to the natural inclination everyone has for what they need. This natural inclination should therefore not be objectionable if what is sought is lawful. On the other hand, the excessive pursuit of passions and desires is dispraised.

If passionate desires are absolutely criticized, it is because most of them are not allowed.

Know that part of our inner self is intellectual whose virtue is wisdom, and its vice is ignorance. Another part is alive and vibrant, its virtue is enthusiasm and its vice is cowardice. A third part is lustful, its virtue lies in chastity and its vice lies in the unrestrained pursuit of passions.

To be patient in the face of evil and temptation is a merit of the soul. So whoever lacks patience and his unlawful desires gain the upper hand, has therefore chosen his passions instead of his intellect (and reasoning) to be the leader. Due to this he risks suffering loss where he hoped to find gain, and he will find suffering where he hoped to find happiness.

In fact, humans were preferred to animals for reasons of common sense (the intellect). Intelligence is designed to curb a person's unlawful desires. So whoever does not accept the judgment of his reason and conforms to that of his passion becomes worse than an animal.

Evidence that proves the excellence of our struggle against passions includes the merits and superiority of hunting dogs over other dogs. This is because of their ability to contradict their instincts, and they therefore keep the prey of their hunt for their master (instead of eating it), either out of fear of punishment or as a token of appreciation.

Know that passions (and unlawful desires) are like the example of the flowing water that guides the ship of a person's nature. Those of a sound mind must understand that in fighting the passions, it is much easier to endure adversity (that results when one fights the temptations of unlawful desires) than to endure what comes after they have satisfied their passions. The least serious condition to expect when blindly following one's desires is that one cannot help but submit to them, even when one is tired of committing them (and he does them without any enjoyment). This is the example for those addicted to sex or alcohol.

Meditating and pondering on this topic makes it easier to reject our evil impulses. When we remember that the purpose of our creation is not to act according to our desires, then passions become repulsive in the eyes of the thinker. Indeed, the camel eats more than a human, the bird copulates more than he does, the desires of the animals are limitless, and unlike humans, they do not repent after they have satisfied them. This therefore proves that man was not created to follow his passionate desires because they are not paramount and are spoiled by the imperfections (of man).

The blameworthy desires (Al-Hawa) are those which go beyond the limits and which our intellect reasons to be flawed.

CHAPTER 3: THE DIFFERENCE BETWEEN THE PERCEPTION OF REASON AND THE PERCEPTION OF PASSION

Passionate desire encourages you to seek pleasure without thinking about the consequences, even after knowing that satisfying that pleasure produces greater suffering than pleasure.

Yet the urge to satisfy the passionate desire distracts from thinking about it and puts the slave of desires in a worse state than that of animals, knowing that animals have an excuse since they (don't have an intellect and) cannot review the consequences of their actions.

A wise person, therefore, cannot exchange a high and noble rank by which he has been honored for a low rank. His reasoning and his intellect must examine the consequences, distinguish between useful and not useful. Reasoning plays the role of the doctor we consult.

Passion is like the ignorant boy or the obese person

who is sick. For this reason, when the intellect can discern the call of inclinations, the wise and sensible person should trust it. In fact, the person should know that their mind and intellect are advising them with knowledge and sincerity. HE must therefore be patient to obey them, for knowledge of their merits is sufficient to benefit them.

If he still needs additional evidence of the superiority of his intelligence, he should ponder the consequences of pursuing passionate desires, such as (leading to) exposing his shameful actions in full view (of others), defamation, or leading him to leave good actions and virtue.

The glories - were they not discredited and the honors despised (by others) when a person pursued his passions?

By reflecting on the (disgusting) condition one feels after doing the sinful desire and the severity of the sin a person gains (when he does the sin), he realizes that one has lost twice by doing the sin.

A poet said on the subject:

How much joy did happiness bring?

(It only) Revealed sadness and pain in the end!

How many times has desires destroyed those who have tasted them!

Know that if man acts according to his passions, in the end he will find shame and humiliation in him. Although his desires do not directly harm him, he feels suffocated by them. But when he gains the upper hand over his inclinations, he regains his honor and pride in himself and feels victorious and triumphant.

It is for this reason that people are so fascinated by ascetics (the knowledgeable people who act on the Quran and Sunnah) that they want to kiss hands (as a sign of respect). This is because they perceive them as people who were strong enough to give up passionate desires (Hawa).

CHAPTER 4: HEALING INSANE LOVE (AL- 'ISHQ)

Passionate love is a disease that has taken its toll on many people, be it in their bodies, their religion, or both.

Anyone who refrains to mix the toxic ingredients of this disease by looking down and lowering the gaze will be saved. Otherwise he'll get as sick as whoever joins this dangerous mix.

If he succeeds in correcting himself before mad passionate love becomes deeply rooted in him, this technique (of looking down and lowering the gaze) can be useful to him. On the other hand, if he allows this disease to take hold in him and the disease has progressed, then this remedy (lowering the gaze) will not be of any use to him.

Know that just looking at what you want doesn't lead directly to passionate love. On the other hand, it often results in the onset of this disease when it is supported by the power of lust, youth and desire.

So if you want to enjoy the cure of lowering your

gaze, you have to hurry before the disease takes root. This will prevent the disease from occurring. Lowering the gaze can only be achieved through blocking and through patience in this struggle to avoid sin. In fact, the most effective treatment is self-control and determination.

The best help in this fight is the fear of **ALLAH** to keep the despicable soul from humiliating itself. One should also remember the flaws and shortcomings of the one with whom he fell madly in love. Ibn Mas'ud said, "If any one of you loves a woman, let him remember her faults."

When the beloved is accessible and lawful to the lover, union (through marriage) becomes the best remedy. The intensity of this disease decreases with marriage, the long journey in life, the thought of being betrayed by the loved one, reading books on self-discipline, remembering death, visiting the diseased, and visiting cemeteries.

There is a story of a man who fell in love with a young person. One day when he looked at himself in the mirror, he noticed gray hair. Then he left the young person.

The young person then wrote to him:

Why was I abandoned like never before?

And the signs of surrender are so clear

And I see you staring at me but confusing me (loving differently than him).

Though I always knew that I was your only love.

The man replied:

I act like a little boy when I'm really old

I am marked with embarrassment

Don't blame me for your disappointment

What I've spent is enough for me

I will be held accountable for what I did

So protect me from the sins I might commit

We saw the father of mankind (Adam)

To be humiliated for a mistake.

Chapter 5: Healing of Gluttony (Al-Shara)

Be aware that the term Al-Shara, when used in a general sense, refers to the passionate consumption of food.

Numerous incidents have been reported of how the greed for food made some suffer.

Al-Harith ibn Kildah said:

"Continuing to eat after you've eaten has killed the wild animals."

Others claimed that if the dead were asked what caused their deaths, they would reply, "satiety."

It was reported that Al-Hasan said that Sumrah was once warned that his son did not sleep at night. Then he asked whether he was eating a lot or not. HE was told that was the case. Then he said, "If he dies, I will not say the funeral prayer over him."

One man said to another to provoke him: "Your father died because he ate too much and your mother died because she drank too much."

'Uqbah Al-Rassibi reports that he entered Al-Hasan's house while he was having lunch.

Al-Hasan insisted on eating with him, so 'Uqbah replied that he was full.

Al-Hasan then said:

"Glory to **ALLAH**! Does the Muslim eat until he is full?"

Excess food

Know that the wise man eats to survive while the ignorant lives to eat. Many bites (of food) prevented other (future) bites by causing (early) death.

The goal here is to channel compulsive eating and preventing it from causing harm.

Al-Sharah (gluttony) also manifests itself in sexual relationships.

This closes the vas deferens and allows unsuitable substances to penetrate. Important organs such as the brain, heart or liver then lose their strength. Sexual desire then decreases and begins to fail faster than normal. In addition, sexual relationship is something that a noble and decent person turns away from. This is the case unless the intent is to have a child or to ward off a pervasive evil (fear of fornication). Except for these cases, when it becomes a habit that is only practiced for pleasure or enjoyment, then one is competing with animals.

The accumulation of wealth

Al-Shara can also refer to the accumulation of money when someone runs after what is beyond their needs. It amounts to madness because money should not be sought for oneself, but rather to acquire useful things. This is what someone does, for example, who collects what he and his children need so that they can avoid begging.

Likewise, it is not to be blamed when giving any of it to those in need. However, the sane is the one who, once he has acquired what is sufficient for him, neither spends his precious time nor risks his priceless soul by crossing lands and seas [to acquire more goods].

How beautiful are the poet's words:

And those who spend their days amassing money for fear of poverty are in fact impoverished.

We have seen and heard many stories of stingy people who, despite their advanced age, traveled and sailed in search of money and profit. They died during their journey without even being able to reach the object of their desire.

Because of this, this disease needs to be treated by understanding what saving is and by finding the balance between making money and risking the most precious possessions one has (such as your time and soul).

That being said, anyone who advises their mind will know what it is meant for. Those who are overwhelmed by the sickness of accumulating money will perish in the desert of desire.

Extravagance

Al-Sharah can also appear in the pleasure of extravagance (magnificent buildings, thoroughbred horses, sophisticated clothing ...).

This disease has its origins in monitoring

passionate desires. Their remedy lies in realizing that the retribution for rightful gain is the grave, that extravagance is forbidden, and that **ALLAH** does not look at those who leave their robes to drag around out of pride.

The wise person is the one who thinks about the time remaining and thinks about his final home. He will then be content with what clothes he is wearing and with his house, which is his accommodation.

It was reported that Noah (peace be upon him) lived in a wool house for 950 years. The PROPHET (peace and blessings of **ALLAH** be upon him) never put one stone on another (his house was of mud). 'Umar ibn Al-Khattab's clothing showed twelve patches. All because they understood that this world is a bridge and that a bridge should not be taken as a home.

Those who do not acquire this knowledge will therefore suffer from the sickness of gluttony. He will then have to take care of (treat) himself by searching for knowledge and consulting the biographies of enlightened scholars.

CHAPTER 6: REJECTION OF A POSITION OF AUTHORITY IN THIS WORLD

Know that our ego urges us to love superiority over others. That is why power is desired, because it makes it possible to command and forbid.

Power and authority, though necessary, involve many risks.

Those who love power and authority must know that they will (only) view them as grandiose until they attain them. Once obtained, they will grow low in his eyes, and then he will strive for something greater. Only after attaining it does the pleasure go away, but the sins remain, as does the risk of losing one's soul and religion. Meditating on this is the remedy for the love of power and authority.

Abu Umamah reports that the PROPHET (peace and blessings of Allaah be upon him) said: "There is no man who does not become the ruler of ten or more people without coming to Allaah with his hands around his neck on the Day of Judgment. His righteousness will set him free or his injustice will destroy him. Its (acquisition of power) beginning is guilt, its middle is regret and its end is decay on Judgment Day."

Abu Dharr reports: "I once asked the Messenger of ALLAH (peace and blessings of ALLAH be upon him): 'Why don't you entrust me with an assignment?' The PROPHET (peace be upon him) patted my shoulder and said:

'O Abu Dharr, you are too weak for this sacred good, which will be humiliation and regret on the day of the resurrection, unless whoever takes it is worthy and fulfills his obligations.'"

In another version: "O Abu Dharr, I see you too weak and I love for you what I love for myself. Don't take responsibility for two people or take charge of the orphan's property."

Chapter 7: Healing Greed

First of all, you must know that honest money saving is not considered greed. Someone may want to set aside money for their needs, for unforeseen events, or for their children and relatives. Whoever does this is considered cautious and there is no reason to blame them. In addition, for some, saving may even improve their situation.

Rather, the term "greed" refers to someone who fails to meet his or her obligations in relation to his or her property. Ibn 'Umar said, "HE who gives [obligatory] alms is not stingy." Likewise, a person is stingy who does not give people what could be of use (to them) without any harm to him.

The PROPHET (peace be upon him) said:

"What disease is as incurable as avarice?"

Abu Muhammad al-Ramharmazi said: "Avarice is like a disease because it harms people, takes honor and provokes revolt. It also weakens the body, satisfies the cravings and changes the skin tone."

The wise used to say, "The generous person is free because he has his money, while the miser does not deserve to be called free because his money owns him."

'Abdullah ibn' Umar (may Allaah be pleased with him) reports that the PROPHET (peace and blessings of Allaah be upon him) said: "Beware of greed, for it destroyed those who lived before you. It ordered them to break the ties of kinship and they did, it ordered them to be stingy and they got stingy, it told them to give in to depravity and they gave in."

HE (peace be upon him) also said: "Two qualities are not combined in the believer: greed and bad morals."

Bishr Al-Hafi said: "Meeting stingy people is an agony for the hearts of believers."

The cure for greed lies in thinking and reflecting. Those who meditate will see that the poor are their brothers. He has been preferred to them [materially] and they need his help. He should therefore thank Him (ALLAH) who blessed him by bringing comfort to his brothers.

Remember that the honor of generosity is also part of the cure. Indeed, generosity can turn the free man (who has received the generosity) into a slave in relation to his benefactor. On the other hand, bad people will do anything to destroy the miserly situation. Anything left in his hands will be uncomfortable for him. Therefore, it is preferable for him to part with it before his property leaves him [for example, by donating his money to good causes before that money is taken away from him].

CHAPTER 8: NOT WASTING

Wasting and squandering wealth is one of the things to which desires invite but which the intellect and reason condemn. The best discipline in this matter is the discipline with which ALLAH advised us:

"And don't spend (your wealth) lavishly like a spendthrift." (Surat al-Isra 26)

Know that a person can get a whole month's sustenance (can be blessed by ALLAH with this provision) in one day. If he spends it thoughtlessly, he will suffer the rest of the month. On the other hand, if he spends it wisely, he will live happily through the end of the month.

The cure for this disease lies in thinking about the consequences of his actions. Likewise, caution about the possibility of future poverty or hardship inhibits the urge to spend thoughtlessly.

CHAPTER 9: CLARIFICATION OF THE AMOUNT OF INCOME AND EXPENDITURE

A wise man's income must exceed his needs. He should also think about saving in case something bad happens. Should problems prevent him from working or earning a living, his savings must be sufficient to meet his needs until the end of his life.

On the other hand, the person whose wife is to give birth, who wants to take another wife or whose child needs money, has to earn a sufficient income to cover these situations.

In general, the expenses should be lower than the income. This way, you can save to deal with the unexpected. In any case, this is what reason demands, as opposed to passionate desire, which is only interested in immediate pleasure.

CHAPTER 10: THE BLAME FOR LYING

Lying is one of the ways that passion calls for because people prefer to be the informant out of love for power and authority. In fact passion knows the superiority of the informant over the informed.

The cure for this disease (lying) is in knowing **ALLAH**'s punishment for the liar. It also is in the firm belief that a person who lies constantly will one day be exposed. He will inevitably be dishonored. His shame grows and no one will respect him enough to believe him, even if he is telling the truth. The mistrust of the people will exceed the size of their lies.

The PROPHET (peace and blessings of **ALLAH** be upon him) said: "Man does not stop lying and endeavors in telling them until he is registered with **ALLAH** as a liar."

Ibn Mas'ud said: "All character traits can be found in the believer except betrayal and lies."

Chapter 11: Protect Yourself From Envy

Envy consists in wishing that the benefit that touched the envied person will disappear even if the envious person does not receive the same benefit. This disease has its roots in a love of distinction and hatred for being like other people. That is why the envious suffers when he notices an advantage in another that distinguishes him from human beings. This distinction, or the fact that the other suddenly becomes equal to the envious one, feeds that suffering. This will only go away when the benefit of the envied person is withdrawn.

It is rare to find someone whose heart is absolutely free from any envy. To have this feeling becomes a sin only when the envious hopes for the disappearance of the blessings granted to his Muslim brother.

Know that cravings cause insomnia, poor diet, paleness, mood swings, and constant depression. A 120-year-old man was asked, "How did you live so long?" He replied, "I let go of envy so I could live a long life."

Know that envy occurs only when it comes to the affairs of this world. You will not find people envying those who pray at night or fast often. Likewise, no one envies scholars for their knowledge. Rather, it is the famous and the rich who are envied.

The first step in curing this disease is to know that what **ALLAH** has ordained will happen. Trying to change fate is impossible. The One who distributes food among men is **ALLAH**. **HE** gives and **HE** withdraws. It is **HE** who created the universe and all that it contains.

By envying it is as if the envious are objecting to the will of the Giver (**HE** be exalted). A wise man said:

"Tell the one who envies me

Do you know who you misbehave towards?

Your bad behavior is towards **ALLAH** in relation to what **HE** gives

Because you are not happy with what **HE** gave me

So **HE** rewarded me for what you did by adding (**HIS** blessings) to me and slamming the doors of livelihood in your face."

Besides, the person envied took nothing of the food of the envious, nor did he take anything from his hands. So if the envious wants another's blessings to disappear then it is clearly an injustice.

The envious should think about the situation of the person he envies. If what he has attained concerns only this lower worldly life, then the envious person should feel compassion rather than jealousy. This is because what the envied one has gained is probably against him and not in his favor (if he has only gained material things in this world). Indeed, the surplus of goods in this lower world is nothing but a source of problems.

Al- Mutanabi said:

"The young man spoke of his life and his need

While the excess of food is nothing but trouble."

This is explained by the fact that the rich are constantly worried about losing their money. If you have a lot of maids, you are always worried about them. The leader fears being sidelined every day. It is therefore necessary to know that the many benefits are accompanied by anxiety.

Moreover, these benefits are temporary and unhappiness follows them. In fact, those who own these benefits are still worried for them thinking that will go away. You should also know that the object of envy is often not as valuable in the eyes of the envied one as it is in the eyes of the jealous.

People think that those who hold important positions are the happiest. In reality, they fail to realize that once these high-ranking people get what they want, they no longer care for this position, and strive for something greater.

Meanwhile, the jealous ones continue to be jealous of them for the same thing (which they don't value).

Let the jealous know that if the person they envied punished them (for their envy), they could not possibly cause them more pain than they are already suffering (because of their envy). So if the jealous person does not manage to heal himself through the counseling mentioned above then he can only be healed by working hard and achieving what he envies.

One of the pious predecessors said: "I am afraid of envy. Indeed, when a man is jealous of his neighbor for his great wealth, he travels to trade, and to get as rich as him. When he envies someone's knowledge, he stays up all night to learn. But people love idleness, they therefore blame the one who has achieved a high rank."

How beautiful are the words of Al-Rida:

"... I am the beautiful and pure white horse

All eyes are on me because

I spend my nights visiting the high ranks while they sleep.

If others did not respect me then

My enemies would not have tried to slander me."

After all that has been said, if the envious person does not get what the envied one has achieved, he will have to fight with his tongue to keep him from slander and lock up the envy he feels in his heart.

There are many hadiths that condemn envy.

The PROPHET (peace and blessings of **ALLAH** be upon him) said: "The sickness of the peoples who preceded you is creeping towards you: the blade of envy and hatred. I'm not talking about what shaves your hair, I'm talking about what religion shaves. Through him, who holds my soul in **HIS** hand, you will only go to heaven if you believe, and you will only believe if you love one another. Would I tell you what, if you do it, will make you love each other? Spread salam among yourselves."

'Umar ibn Maymun said: Musa (peace be upon him) saw a man on the throne, so he envied him [that is, he loved what he saw and wished for it, for himself, without wanting to take advantage of this man] and asked people about him. They said, "Would you like to know more about his works? **HE** does not envy people what **ALLAH** has given them by His grace, he does not participate in bad talk and he does not disobey his parents."

The PROPHET (peace and blessings of Allaah be upon him) said: "Envy is only allowed in two cases: a man whom Allaah has given knowledge of the Quran and who reads it day and night, and a man whom Allaah has given a fortune which he justly spends day and night."

CHAPTER 12: HEALING GRUDGES

Resentment arises from the traces that bad deeds and bad words of people leave on the ego of the angry person. In fact, it is the mind of a person that decides whether the traces of bad or good deeds of others will stay in his mind.

'Abdullah ibn Ka'b ibn Malik reported that he had heard the story of Ka'b ibn Malik, that he did not accompany the PROPHET (peace and blessings of Allaah be upon him) to Tabuk, as well as the account of the time of the revelation of the acceptance of his repentance. Ka'b said: "At last I entered the mosque and the MESSENGER of ALLAH (peace and blessings of ALLAH be upon him) was sitting among the people. Talhah ibn Ubaydillah shook my hand and congratulated me." Ka'b never forgot this sign of friendship with Talha (Allah be pleased with them both).

This proves that good deeds and favors are never forgotten, just like bad deeds. Even so, it is best to try to erase all traces of resentment from your heart. The cure for this evil (of resentment) is found in forgiveness.

Forgiveness is divided into two phases:

The first is to remember the reward given to the forgiver (by Allah).

The second is to thank the One who made it possible for us to forgive the one who made the mistake.

The perfection of forgiveness is achieved through contentment and satisfaction. This can only be done by releasing from the heart all resentment towards the other.

A more specific remedy is to remember the fact that when one is touched by an evil, it is the result of a sin committed by him, or that it is intended to purify or improve his rank, or to test his or her patience.

A person should know that everything that reaches him comes from the One Who Predestines.

CHAPTER 13: PROTECTION FROM EXCESSIVE ANGER

Anger is part of human nature and it helps ward off danger and defends you against attackers.

There are some disliked aspects to excessive anger, however. Anger disturbs reason and causes imbalance and excess. In this way, the victim of anger begins to make bad decisions that may affect him more than those they are angry at.

Anger is a fire that spreads when something provokes it. It boils the blood with rage and can even cause a fever.

The main reason for anger is arrogance. This is because a person is rarely angry with someone who is above them (in position and status).

The cure (of this disease) is for the angry person to change his state. If he is talking, he should become silent. If he's standing, let him sit down. When he's seated, have him lie down. All of this is recommended so that he can regain his calm.

If he immediately changes his location and leaves the location, that's better. He should also remember the merit of controlling his anger; for **ALLAH** has praised this.

"Those who spend in ease and adversity, who suppress their anger and forgive others." (Ali Imran 134)

Also, make the person who is angry to think about whether this is happening to him because of a sin he has committed or whether it was predetermined for him. Then he will find his anger becoming less.

Many hadiths have been recorded on the subject of anger.

According to Abu Hurayrah (may **ALLAH** be pleased with him):

"A man asked the PROPHET (peace and blessings of **ALLAH** be upon him):

- "Give me some advice."

- "Do not get angry." replied the PROPHET (peace and blessings of **ALLAH** be upon him).

The man repeated the request several times and the PROPHET (peace and blessings of ALLAH be upon him) repeated his answer."

The PROPHET (peace and blessings of ALLAH be upon him) said: "The strong is not the one who rules others with his strength, but the strong is the one who controls himself in anger."

Soulayman ibn Surad (may Allaah be pleased with him) reports that he was at the side of the PROPHET (peace and blessings of Allaah be upon him) when two men began to exchange names. One of them had a red face and tight arteries in his throat. The PROPHET (peace and blessings of ALLAH be upon him) said, "I know a word that would calm this man. If he said, 'I seek refuge in ALLAH from Satan the accursed, he would get rid of what he feels."

The PROPHET (peace and blessings of Allaah be upon him) said: "If any of you is angry, let him sit down to cast his anger out. If it doesn't leave him, let him go to bed."

Al-Khattabi said, "The one who is standing is more

likely to move and hurt someone than the one who is sitting."

The PROPHET (peace and blessings of ALLAH be upon him) said: "If any one of you is angry, let him be silent."

Al-Ahnaf said, "What prevents an angry person from controlling himself is nothing but the evil of hurry."

If an angry person does not calm down at the height of their anger, they can harm themselves or the person they are angry with. After that, he will surely regret what he did.

Many people were killed and injured because of anger, and those who committed these evil deeds out of anger were consumed with regret for the rest of their lives. Excessive anger also harms the person who is feeling it.

A man was once very angry to the point of screaming. Suddenly he spat blood and died instantly. Another man hit someone he was angry with and broke his own fingers in the process. The victim, however, suffered no harm.

In order to heal themselves, the person experiencing excessive anger needs to remember their state when they are angry and their state when they are calm. Then he will understand that anger is a state of madness and excess. If the angry person is still determined to attack their target, ask them to change their state (sitting, standing, etc.). Then he will realize the ugliness of the act he was about to do. He will therefore choose to abandon his plan.

When our pious predecessors got angry, they often forgave in search of the merit of satisfaction. Some among them thought that this anger was a result of their sins. Others thought it was a test.

It is reported that in some ancient revealed books ALLAH said: "O son of Adam! Think of Me when you are angry, I will remember you when you commit a sin so that I don't destroy you with those I would destroy. If you have been wronged, be satisfied with My support, for My support is better for you than your own victory."

Mawriq said, "I never said a word when angry that I did not regret after calming down."

Ibn 'Awn never got angry. When a man provoked him, he replied, "May **ALLAH** bless you."

A person who is angry at another should never chastise him while he is angry, even if he deserves chastisement. Rather, he must wait until he has calmed down so that the chastisement corresponds to the offense suffered and is not exaggerated because of his anger.

A man who was angry with 'Umar ibn' Abd Al-'Aziz was brought to him. Then he said to him, "If I hadn't been angry with you, I would have hit you." Then he let him go without punishing him.

CHAPTER 14: HEALING PRIDE

The proud one brags and despises others. Arrogance arises from a feeling of superiority over those who are inferior in, for example, parentage, possessions, knowledge, or worship. The signs of arrogance are shown in the contempt of those who feel superior to you. Sometimes it also means (a person's) boastful gait, excessive pride, and a love of compliments.

The cure for this disease is based on two approaches: a general approach and a specific approach.

The general approach to its treatment is divided into two aspects: theoretical and practical.

The theoretical aspect relies on textual and logical evidence that shows the shortcomings of arrogance. The practical part is hanging out with humble people and listening to their stories.

The specific approach is achieved through meditating on our failing nature. Those who are proud of their money should know that it will soon be taken away. He should also realize that excellence consists in being satisfied with something and not needing it. Those who take pride in their knowledge should realize that there are many more learned than he who preceded him in this search. In addition, his knowledge prevents him from being arrogant. What he is proud of therefore becomes evidence against him. After all, if the reason for his excessive pride is a good deed, then he knows it is a mistake, not an honor, to ponder and think that it is perfect.

'Abdullah ibn' Amr met Ibn 'Umar on Mount Marwah. They then discussed during the descent. 'Abdullah ibn' Amr later went away. Ibn 'Umar then sat down and wept. He was asked, "Why are you crying?"

He replied: "He ('Abdullah ibn' Amr) claims that he heard the Messenger of ALLAH (peace be upon him) say: 'Whoever has the weight of an atom of pride in his heart, ALLAH will throw him into hell on his own face."

Ilyas ibn Salamah reports that his father said:

"The Messenger of ALLAH (peace and blessings of

ALLAH be upon him) said: "A man glorifies himself until he is inscribed under the tyrants, then he endures what has hit them."

According to Abdallah bin Mas'ud, the PROPHET (peace be upon him) said: "Whoever has the weight of an atom of pride in his heart will not go to Heaven."

A man asked, "What about a man who likes to wear nice clothes and nice shoes?" "

HE (peace and blessings of ALLAH be upon him) replied, "ALLAH is beautiful and loves beauty. (Being) Proud is to reject the truth and look down on others."

The PROPHET (peace and blessings of Allaah be upon him) [reported that Allaah said]: "Pride is My cloak and glory is my lower garment. Anyone who argues (competes) with me about it, I will torment him."

Al-Khattabi said, "It means that pride and greatness are two attributes that only characterize ALLAH. Nobody shares it with Him. No created person deserves to own it, for the created thing is characterized by subservience and lowliness. ALLAH has chosen the cloak and undergarment as examples, since no one shares his cloak and undergarment with any other person. Likewise, ALLAH shares neither His pride nor His greatness with anyone and only ALLAH knows. "

Al-Khattabi also said: "And his word 'whoever has the weight of an atom of pride in his heart will not go to heaven' can have two meanings. The first is that it refers to the pride of disbelief. The second is that HE (ALLAH) removes pride from the hearts of those who enter Paradise. His word 'despise others' means to look down on them and bring them down."

Al-Hasan said, "You can see people exaggeratingly praise a man who says to him, 'You are so and so,' and then he sits in silence and believes everything he is told. And you see a man walking slowly and presumptuously instead of walking in the usual way."

CHAPTER 15: HEALING VANITY

Vanity arises from the love we have for ourselves. In fact, we never notice the flaws of the one we love, and we refuse to distinguish his flaws. The lover sees only perfection in what he loves.

The consequence of vanity is to hate the thing that caused it. This is because the conceited person does not seek progress in himself but searches for the mistakes of others.

The cure for vanity is knowing what your faults are. To do this, the patient person should ask his friends about his mistakes and think about the condition of his predecessors, who were affected by the same disease as him.

The scholar who is infatuated with his knowledge should read the biographies of the scholars of past generations. Let the conceited ascetics consult the biographies of the ascetics in front of them. This will make his excessive pride go away. Imam Ahmed knew more than a million hadiths by heart, and Kahmas ibn al-Hasan recited the entire Quran three times a day. Salman al-Taymi prayed al-Fajr with the same ablutions as the al-'Isha prayer for forty years.

Anyone who thinks about other people's lives will understand that compared to them, he is like the man who owns a dinar. He's so proud of it that he doesn't realize that there are people with thousands and thousands of dinars.

Ibrahim al-Khawas said: "Vanity prevents one from knowing one's capabilities and limits."

A sage once said: "A person's self-sufficiency is an enemy of his intellectual faculties. How harmful is vanity to honors!"

CHAPTER 16: HEALING FROM BOASTING (AL-RIYA')

Anyone who really knows **ALLAH** will sincerely devote all their worship to Him. Indeed, boasting and showing off occur in someone who does not know his Creator well, who does not glorify **ALLAH** as he should, and who seeks praise and compliments from people.

There are different categories of people who are affected by this disease. Some just seek praise from others. Others seek **ALLAH**'s satisfaction as well as praise. Still others hope for no praise, but when they notice that they are being watched, such as praying, they put even more diligence into their prayer (to show off). In this case, it is a defect that interferes with the good act itself.

The general cure of this disease lies in the true knowledge of **ALLAH**. In fact, the one who knows Him will devote all his worship to Him and will not consider anyone but Him. **HE** will put himself in the position of a humble worshiper. It must be remembered that reward is given only on the basis of righteous works. He must therefore be careful not to waste his efforts unnecessarily (by doing actions for others instead of **ALLAH**).

He also needs to know that the penalty for boasting is harsh.

The PROPHET (peace and blessings of Allaah be upon him) said: "Actions are worthy only by their intentions, and everyone is rewarded only according to their intentions."

According to Abu Musa, a Bedouin asked the PROPHET (peace be upon him): "O Messenger of **ALLAH**, which of these men is fighting in **ALLAH**'s way? The one who fights for the booty, (the one) who fights for fame, or (the one) who fights to show his importance? (One version mentions): The one who fights out of bravery or the one who fights out of partisan spirit? Another version mentions: The one who fights out of anger? The PROPHET (peace and blessings of Allaah be upon him) replied: "Whoever fights for the word of Allaah to be the highest, fights in the way of Allaah."

According to Abu Hurairah (may **ALLAH** be pleased with him), the PROPHET (peace be upon him) said: "The first men to be judged on the Day of Judgment will certainly be:

- A man who died a martyr. He will be brought and **ALLAH** will make him acknowledge His blessings and he will acknowledge them. **ALLAH** will say, "What did you do with these blessings?"

He will answer, "I fought for you until I died a martyr."

ALLAH will then say, "You are lying, you preferred to fight to be said (by the people) that you were brave and that is what has been said."

Then **ALLAH** will order that he be pulled over his face until he is thrown into the fire.

- A man who has learned knowledge, taught and recited the Quran will be brought and **ALLAH** will make him acknowledge His blessings and he will recognize them.

ALLAH will say, "What did you do with these blessings?"

He will answer: "I have learned knowledge, I have

taught it and I have read the Quran - all for you."

ALLAH will then say, "You are lying, you are more likely to have learned knowledge so that they say that you are a scholar and you read the Quran so that they say that you are a reciter and all that has been said."

Then ALLAH will order that he be pulled over his face until he is thrown into the fire.

- A man to whom ALLAH has given His gifts and to whom HE has given all kinds of goods will be brought and ALLAH will make him acknowledge His blessings and he will acknowledge them. ALLAH will say, "What did you do with these blessings?"

He will reply, "I've spent money on every thing you wanted it to be spent on."

ALLAH will then say, "You are lying, you preferred to spend to be said (by the people) that you were generous and that was said."

Then ALLAH will order that he be pulled over his face until he is thrown into the fire.

The PROPHET (peace and blessings of ALLAH be upon him) said: "ALLAH said: I have the greatest right not to have a partner. So whoever worships for someone else leads to associating with ME, I will deny him and leave him with whoever he associated ME with."

It is reported that the PROPHET (peace and blessings of ALLAH be upon him) said: "What I fear most for you is minor shirk!"

HE was asked, "O MESSENGER of ALLAH, what is it?"

HE (peace and blessings of ALLAH be upon him) replied, "Al-Riya".

ALLAH, Exalted be HE, will say on Judgment Day after rewarding people for their works:

"Go to those who used to show off their good deeds and see if they got any rewards."

Ibn Tawbah Abu Ja'far 'Abdullah said:

"In a dream after his death, I saw Abu Bakr Al-Adami, the reciter, begging. I said to him, "What has **ALLAH** done to you?"

He replied: "I stood before him and endured a lot of suffering."

I then said to him: "And what about the nights (spent in worship), good works and the **Quran** ?!"

He replied, "There was nothing worse for me because I did these actions for life down here!"

So I said to him, "What happened to you?"

He replied: "**ALLAH**, may **HE** be Exalted, said to me: I made it a point never to torture anyone who turns 80 years old."

CHAPTER 17: HEALING FROM EXCESSIVE THINKING

Know that thinking is needed to remember what has been forgotten and to think about what might be beneficial in the future. However, unnecessary thinking is harmful and if overdone, it tires the body.

The hypocrites say, "Scholars should stop thinking every now and then before they exhaust their bodies." But the reality is that a wise person should not stop thinking about what he can achieve. However, when the layperson envisions becoming caliph, or as learned as Abu Hanifah or Al Shafi'i,

or as ascetic as Bishr al-Hafi and Ma'ruf al-Karkhi, or that he has the fortune of 'Abdul-Rahman ibn 'Awf, then by these thoughts he tires his body. This is especially true if he is just imagining and doing nothing (instead of working hard to get what he wants). Rather, everyone should think about what is available to them and what good works they can achieve. Likewise, he has to think about his fight against the devil.

Ibn 'Abbas said, "It is better to pray two units with

reverence than to pray all night with distracted hearts."

Umm Al-Darda was asked, "What was Abu Al-Darda's best deed?"

She replied: "Contemplation and meditation."

Malik ibn Dinar stood praying until dawn and said: "The people of the fire did not stop presenting themselves to me in chains and with an iron collar until dawn."

Some wise men said, "Chasing thinking leads to blindness."

CHAPTER 18: HEALING FROM EXCESSIVE SADNESS

Know that a healthy person's heart cannot be spared from sadness. In fact, the memory of his sins makes him sad. Then he thinks of his negligence and ponders the words of the learned and the pious and regrets not following them.

Malik ibn Dinar said, "The heart without sorrow will be devastated, just as a house without an inhabitant will be devastated."

Ibrahim ibn 'Issa said: "I have never seen anyone so sad as Al-Hasan; Every time I saw him, I said to myself that he had just been touched by a test. "

Malik ibn Dinar said: "The more you mourn for this world, the less fear of Judgment Day dwells in your heart."

Just as sadness seems to accompany the hearts of the virtuous, it should be known that its excess should be avoided.

It was mentioned in a hadith: "The rest of the believer's life is priceless because he can make up for what he has missed." If the sadness is about something that cannot be caught up, then it is of no use. On the other hand, when it comes to religion, one must try to make amends by hoping for the Grace and Mercy of ALLAH.

The loser, on the other hand, will obviously be the one who is saddened by what has been missing in this lower worldly life. A sane person has to get rid of that.

The best cure for sadness is to remind yourself that it is impossible to get back what has been lost. Worse still, being sad adds a second calamity to what we are already experiencing. It is not appropriate to weigh down the ordeal with sadness, but to ease it by pushing it away. Ibn 'Amr said, "When ALLAH takes something away from you, deal (and distract yourself) with something that prevents you from thinking about it." It also makes it easier to think about what ALLAH has given you rather than what HE has taken from you. However, if nothing can alleviate it, then the mourner must struggle to clear his heart of pain.

Know that excessive sadness and grief take root in passionate desires (Hawa), and not in the rational mind. In fact, the intellect refuses to deal with things like excessive sadness that are unnecessary and not useful.

Everyone should know that their affairs will get easier with time. He must therefore endeavor to hasten the coming of what is to happen (i.e., comfort) so that he can ease himself for the duration of the trial until liberation and comfort come to him.

Some of the things that make sadness and grief go away include:

To know that they are useless and believe in the future reward.

Remembering those who have been hit by major disasters.

CHAPTER 19: HEALING FROM SORROWS AND WORRIES

Sadness arises from thinking about the past, while worry arises from fear of the future.

Grief over past sins is beneficial because one is rewarded for it.

Likewise, someone preoccupied with a good job they want to do (in the future) should know that their concern regarding this will be beneficial to them.

One who regrets something about this lower world that has escaped him should remember that what has been missed will not return and it is harmful to regret. It just adds pain to the pain.

The firm and determined person is the one who protects himself from worry, that is, from the loss of something he loves. Hence, one who has many things to cling to will find his worry growing.

The less he has of things that are important to him, the less worries their will be.

The pain caused by not having something is less than a tenth of what someone experiences who has lost something that is dear to them. Haven't you seen that the one who suffers from not having children is in less pain than the one who has lost a child? In addition, a person gets used to enjoying something he loves for a long time until it inhabits his heart. Once lost, the pain felt surpasses any pleasure felt up to that point. This is explained by the fact that the object of love, for example, as well as his health, is an integral part of the human being. As a result, a person finds satisfaction only in possession of the object while its absence bothers him. That's why we suffer more from our loss of the things under our possessions. Our nature believes that what we had was thanks to us.

Therefore, sensible people need to be close to the object of their love in order to maintain some balance. However, when this reaches the level of deep concern, he should strengthen his belief in predestination. Let him remember that what ALLAH has ordained will undoubtedly happen so that he can heal. Let him know that this life is based on suffering. All buildings will end in ruins, all gatherings will end in partings.

The one who wishes that what is destined to disappear to remain is like the one who wishes that what does not exist to exist. So don't let life ask for anything other than what it was created for.

A poet said:

"It [life down here] is only based on suffering and yet you want it free from all prejudice and pain."

On the other hand, if a person imagines that they have suffered greater suffering than what actually happened, then their real suffering will be easier to bear. This is because the good porters have a habit of putting something heavy on what they are carrying. After they get used to the load, they take the heavy item off and that makes their actual load lighter in their eyes.

In good times, everyone should expect that a trial will come at some point. This makes him think about what he's going to keep instead of what he's going to lose. So if a less serious misfortune hits him, he will endure it more easily. Like someone who loses his money and sees what is left as profit. Or like someone who imagined the loss of his eyesight, a poor eyesight will then be more bearable, as will any other less serious illness.

A poet said:

The clever one introduces himself

(That he is) Touched by trials before they touch him.

(Then) their sudden arrival,

Doesn't surprise him because he'd already considered it.

And the ignorant trust his day

And forgets the death of those who came before him.

Then when the trials come they surprise him

A couple of misfortunes are enough to lose him.

If he'd been tough on himself

Patience would have taught him courage.

One of the pious predecessors said:

I saw a woman who surprised me with her youth.

I said, "That face has never seen grief or sadness."

She replied, "Don't say that, because I don't know anyone who has suffered as I have suffered. I had a husband who brought an animal to sacrifice. I had two sons. The elder said to his brother, "Come on, I'll show you how our father sacrificed the sheep." Then he slaughtered his brother. When we looked for him, he fled and my husband died trying to catch up with him."

I then said to him: "How do you manage to endure your pain?"

She replied, "If I could find support in grief, I would have used it."

CHAPTER 20: HEALING FROM FEAR OF DEATH AND OVERCAUTIOUSNESS.

Fear and caution relate to future events. One with determination prepares for what he fears. However, he avoids excessive fear of what will inevitably hit him, because such excessive fear is not beneficial to him.

In fact, the fear of **ALLAH** is so strong in the hearts of some virtuous people that they asked Him to diminish it. There is a reason to make this kind of request to **ALLAH**. Because fear is like a whip; If the camel is beaten all the time, it will worry. Rather, the whip should be used when he is lazy, to motivate him to keep going.

It is reported that Sufyan Al-Thawri asked a young man who was sitting with him, "Do you want to sincerely and rightly fear **ALLAH**?"

The young man replied: "Yes".

So Sufyan said to him, "You are a fool! If you fear

ALLAH as you should, you will not even be able to perform the obligatory actions!"

A reasonable person should not be unduly afraid of the disease, as it will inevitably affect him throughout his life. Fear of the inevitable only adds harm to harm. The case is more difficult with regard to the fear of death and worrying about it.

Remembering that death is inevitable makes that thought more bearable, as does the reminder that excessive caution only provides extra caution without bringing any benefit.

Whenever a person tries to imagine the intensity of death it is as if he is experiencing it, but in an emotional way. Therefore, he shouldn't represent it in his head, because he will not die several times, but only once. So if you don't think about it, you alleviate the fear of its coming.

Everyone should also know that **ALLAH** can make death easy if **HE** wants. But what is after death is far more disturbing than death itself. In fact, death is just a bridge that leads us to our eternal home. Therefore, it is appropriate to think of death often in order to do righteous deeds until the day it occurs, rather than just to imagine it.

If the thought of leaving this life makes the heart sad, the healing is in knowing that this world is not a home of joy. Rather, happiness and joy lie in leaving it. Because of this, it is not appropriate to compete to acquire it.

So the wise person is the one who is sad to leave this life only because he can no longer do good deeds in it. This explains why the pious predecessors were also grieved by death.

When Mu'adh ibn Jabal was about to die, he said, "O ALLAH! I feared you, but today my hope lies in you. You know, I didn't like life on earth and didn't want to stay here long. But what I liked was being thirsty in heat waves, showing endurance for hours, and sitting in study circles with scholars."

Those who are struck by death must know that this is a time of great suffering. He will be in deep pain. He will be separated from all the things he loves and the people he loves. He will suffer the horror of agony and fear for the future of his property. This is when the devil comes to try to dissatisfy the servant with his master. He will say to him: "Look at you! What killed you? Isn't it painful? You leave your wife and children and are about to be buried!"

His purpose and aim is for the servant to have a bad opinion of his **LORD**, to hate the orders of **ALLAH**, to protest, to be unjust in the distribution of his inheritance, and so on. In this case, it is necessary to heal yourself from the breaths of the devil and the soul.

The PROPHET (peace and blessings of **ALLAH** be upon him) said: "I seek refuge with **YOU** from the domination of Shaitan at the time of my death."

At that moment Shaitan says to his allies: "If he escapes you now, you will never be able to catch him again." Whoever remembers **ALLAH** in good health, **ALLAH** will protect him when he is sick, and whoever keeps **ALLAH** in mind, **ALLAH** protects his body when he moves.

Ibn 'Abbas reports that the PROPHET (peace and blessings of **ALLAH** be upon him) said: "Pay attention to **ALLAH**, **HE** will pay attention to you. Pay attention to **ALLAH**, you will find **HIM** before you. Remember **HIM** in peace, **HE** will remember you in trouble."

The righteous actions of the Prophet Yunus (peace

be upon him) enabled him to escape the ordeal that had befallen him.

ALLAH, Exalted be HE, said of the Prophet Yunus:

"If he had not been one of those who glorify ALLAH, he would have remained in the belly (of the fish) until the day of resurrection." (as - Saffat 143-144)

Pharaoh did not do a good deed. Then at the time of his ordeal he found nothing to cling to. That is why he was told:

"Well (you believed)? While you used to disobey and were one of the corrupters!" (Yunus 91)

Abdul-Samad, the ascetic, said on his deathbed: "O my LORD! This is the moment I kept YOU (kept YOUR Mercy until this moment). Anyone who was negligent in good health will be neglected during their illness."

It is reported that one of the companions saw an old man begging. Then he said, "This man disobeyed ALLAH's commands in his youth, so ALLAH neglected him when he got old."

The cure for this disease is to encourage the soul, to convince it that it (death) is only for a short time and will pass and then it will experience eternal rest, as the PROPHET (peace and blessings of Allaah be upon him) said: "No anguish will touch your father after this day. "

Al-Mu'tamir ibn Sulayman said: "My father said to me: 'Oh my son! Read for me the hadith that speaks about the concessions of ALLAH so that I may meet HIM in the hope of the best of HIM."

The believer must therefore suppress fear and guide the camel, as one desert camel driver said:

His camel driver told him good news and said

Tomorrow you will see the acacias and the mountains

The PROPHET (peace and blessings of ALLAH be upon him) said [ALLAH said], "I am as my servant thinks of me."

Jabir reports: "I heard the Messenger of ALLAH (peace be upon him) say three days before his death: Do not let any of you die without having a good opinion of **ALLAH**!"

Al-Fudayl ibn 'lyad said, "Fear is better than hope. On the other hand, hope will be better when death comes."

Fear is a whip that encourages the lazy. But when the camel is tired, forbearance should be exercised.

If one asks why 'Umar ibn' Abdul-'Aziz was so afraid at the time of his death, one must answer that his fear was the result of his sense of responsibility and his desire to always respect the rights of all.

He used to say, "Certainly I am afraid of this position of authority!" When Ibn 'Abbas said to him, "Receive the announcement of good news, O Commander of the Faithful! You were given a position of authority, you were righteous and you died a martyr!" He replied, "Oh Ibn 'Abbas! Will you testify to this before **ALLAH**?"

As the dying person's suffering increases, he must see it as a reward. The pious predecessors regarded the intensity of the agony of a sick person as atonement for sins and were pleased with it. One of them reportedly said, "They loved to suffer at the time of death."

It is also reported that 'Umar ibn' Abdul 'Aziz said: "I do not want to be spared the agony of death, for it is the last thing that atones for the sins of the Muslim."

The dying man must repent while he is still clear so that he may meet **ALLAH** cleansed from all sin. He must also write his last wishes and rely on **ALLAH**, the Exalted, for the care of his wife and children, for **HE** supports and protects the virtuous.

If Shaitan bothers him when dying and reminds him of his wasting, let him know that the boat will wither when the traveler leaves it. He should also remember that Sharia law prescribes that after death the believer will live a life of eternal joy. So whoever has a firm belief should not be sad because their destination is good.

It is reported that the PROPHET (peace and blessings of Allaah be upon him) said: "The soul of the Muslim is like a bird that sits on the trees of Paradise until Allaah sends it back to his body."

The aim of this chapter is to show that the fear of

death must be alleviated so that it does not exhaust the body and is not harmful. Rather, we should fear what comes after death and work to prepare for it.

CHAPTER 21: HEALING FROM EXCESSIVE JOY

As the pleasure becomes intensified and excessive, the blood warms up and then it can harm the body and even cause death if not controlled.

The one who finds the means to get happiness should get it. When Yusuf (peace be upon him) met his (younger) brother, he said to him: "Do you have a father?" And he continued to be lenient with him (his brother) so as not to surprise him with the good news (that Yusuf his elder brother was alive and in front of him).

Joy needs to be regulated to match sadness. Its exaggeration is a sign of deep heedlessness. Because joy is not a sign of reason for a healthy person, because when he is happy about something, he remembers his fate and is afraid of his ultimate fate. This is when his joy disappears.

When the recklessness of joy increases, it leads to heedlessness. That is why ALLAH said:

"For ALLAH does not love those who are exultant."

(Qasas 76)

It refers to those who through excessive cheering have exceeded the limits of joy.

The cure for excessive joy lies in deep reflection on the sins committed and the trials to come.

Al-Hasan Al-Basri said, "Death has revealed this lower world. It left the sane with no happiness."

CHAPTER 22: HEALING FROM LAZINESS

A love of leisure, a preference for idleness, and the perceived difficulty of any task are all elements that lead to laziness.

The PROPHET (peace be upon him) said:

"I seek refuge in ALLAH from fear, sadness, old age and laziness."

The PROPHET (peace be upon him) said: "The strong believer is better and more loved by ALLAH than the weak believer. Try every moment to get what is good for you, seek the help of ALLAH and do not be helpless. If something happens to you, don't say, 'If I had just done this or that, it would have happened.' Instead, say, 'It is ALLAH's decree and HE will do what HE wills.' For the words 'if only' opens the door to the devil."

Ibn Mas'ud said, "I hate to see a man being lazy in pursuit of this world or the next."

HE also said, "At the end of time there will be people whose best deeds are criticizing one another, also known as the lazy one's."

Ibn 'Abbas said, "Slackening married laziness and they produced poverty."

Malik ibn Dinar said, "There is no good deed without an obstacle. He who overcomes it with patience will find consolation, but if he fears it, he will refrain from it."

The cure for laziness is to motivate and encourage effort out of fear of missing the mark, of being blamed, or of living with regret. Indeed, the regret of the lazy when he sees the reward of the hardworking, is his greatest punishment. Hence, the reasonable person must ponder the negative consequences of laziness, for leisure has often led to regret.

The one who sees his neighbor coming home from a profitable trip will feel far greater regret than the joy of lazy entertainment, as will be the regret of the lazy student toward the one who attains a high place in the world .

The purpose of these examples is to explain that the frustration of failure exceeds the joy of being lazy.

Wise people agree that wisdom cannot be achieved through relaxation or idleness. Thus, one who knows the consequences of laziness will avoid it, and one who sees the fruits of hard work will endure the difficulties of this path. In addition, the intelligent man knows that he was not created for nothing. On the contrary, in this world he is like a worker or a trader.

The life down here in this world was given to us to do good works. This life and the life in the grave are such short moments compared to eternity in heaven or in hell.

One of the best remedies against laziness is to read the biographies of those who have worked hard and ponder those stories. That is why I (Ibn Jawzi) am amazed at someone who chooses idleness during the sowing season and foregoing profits during the harvest season.

Farqad reportedly said, "You put on your leisure clothes before you even started working. Have you ever noticed that when the worker starts his work, he puts on his most humble clothes? Then, when he's finished, he washes himself and puts on two clean clothes. You put on your casual clothes before you even started to work."

CHAPTER 23: KNOWING YOUR MISTAKES

Know that the self is a loved one. Therefore the mistakes of the loved one cannot appear to the lover's eyes. However, some show such determination in fighting themselves that they consider themselves an enemy. Only then they will be able to realize their mistakes and flaws.

Iyas ibn Mu'awiyah said:

"If you don't know your mistakes, you're a fool!"

Then he was asked, "What are yours?"

He replied, "Too much talk."

However, this case is very rare. In fact, people tend to hide their mistakes. We do not imply that a person is ignorant of their shortcomings, for the healthy one knows how to recognize them. Rather, we are talking about hiding them. They then become internal diseases that the doctor cannot recognize and cure because he cannot recognize symptoms.

In fact, a person's love for himself prevents him from seeing his hidden faults as faults.

A poet said:

The eye of contentment sees no imperfections,

But the eye of discontent sees all flaws.

It is reported that one man was in the company of another and when he was about to leave he said to him:

"Tell me about my mistakes."

The other replied: "Ask someone else because I looked at you with a satisfied eye."

If we ask how a person can recognize his faults when he does not see them as such, we will answer that there are seven ways to achieve this:

1- Whoever is concerned must choose the smartest and most sensible of his friends and ask them to inform him of his mistakes. He has to tell them that they are doing him a favor. Then, when his friend replies to his request, he should be happy about it and not show sadness so as not to keep him from speaking. He should even tell him: "If you are hiding something, I would call you a cheat."

2- He has to ask his neighbors, his brothers and everyone he interacts with what they like and dislike about him.

3- He must learn what his enemies say about him because an enemy is always trying to find his opponent's faults. With this in mind, it becomes possible to take advantage of your enemy in ways that you couldn't even duplicate with a friend. This is because the enemy mentions the flaws while the friend hides them. This opens up the possibility of avoiding these errors.

4- He has to imagine someone else with the same character traits as him. He will then have to keep what he values and give up what is reprehensible.

5- He should meditate on the fruits and consequences of his different personality traits. He will then distinguish the good that results from his good side and the bad that results from his bad side. Honest analysis is powerful and insightful indeed.

6- He must measure his works in the light of Sharia law, have them examined by discerning people and measure them on the scale of justice, all of this in order to distinguish the good from the bad.

7- He must read the stories of those who acted in accordance with their knowledge and he must compare his works with theirs. He will have to view the effects of his mistakes as loopholes to be avoided.

CHAPTER 24: HEALING INACTION

When idleness has become a deeply ingrained habit in the soul, no healing will work on it. On the other hand, if it was acquired through being with lazy people or through the preponderance of desires, then its healing can be achieved in several ways.

Among them, to move away from inactive lazy people and treat them with contempt, and to bond with active people.

The idle should ponder the consequences and fate of those who did little, and compare them with the fate of those who were earnest and hardworking.

As Abdul-Samad said, "A man known for his hard work died while people were saying to him, 'Die today, that you may live forever,' and that saying woke me up."

Anyone who carefully observes generous and hardworking people will find that they are no different from him. He was made like them. They are people like him. Except that the love of idleness and entertainment hurt and tied him up. So they moved on and he stayed. If he had moved his foot with determination, he would have achieved what they have achieved.

A poet said:

If you love a person's character traits, then imitate them and you will become what you loved.

Because there is nothing in the way of generosity and good characters when you approach them.

Anyone who consults the biographies and reports of their pious predecessors will find that most of the scholars and lawyers were among the slaves, the weak and the petty workers. But thanks to their great commitment, they succeeded.

If lazy people pondered the consequences of their inaction, they would understand that their laziness is their enemy. However, they preferred inactivity and rushed towards relaxation and entertainment.

Also, regret for missing out on the greatest virtues due to idleness and the disdain of people, and humiliation are worse than any other ordeal or misfortune.

In contrast, productive people have found solace in encouragement and the elevation of their status in this world and in the hereafter. It gave them relief in the times of adversity they went through. It is as if those who endured the suffering of exertion never relaxed, and those who relaxed never experienced the suffering of exertion.

According to Anas (may Allaah be pleased with him) the PROPHET (peace and blessings of Allaah be upon him) said: "One of the inhabitants of Paradise who has gone through most of the trials in the life of this earth will come to the day of resurrection and it will be said: 'Immerse him once in paradise', then he will be immersed there.

Then **ALLAH** will say: "O son of Adam! Have you seen any difficulties or things that you hate in the past?"

Then he will reply, "No, by your power I have never seen anything I hated."

Then one of the people of Hell who has had the most joys in life here (in the world) will be bought and it is said:

"Immerse him in hell once." Then he is immersed into it.

Then **ALLAH** will say, "O son of Adam, have you seen anything good or thing in the past that pleased your eye?"

Then he will say, "No, by your strength I have never seen anything good, nor anything that pleased my eye."

This hadith means that fatigue and adversity of a believer will one day end and only calm remains. For the unbeliever, one day calm and lightness will disappear and only repentance will remain. In fact, life is only one season of the year, eternal defeat has not yet been recorded, but harvest day is coming soon and that is enough to wake up the lazy.

CHAPTER 25: SELF-DISCIPLINE

Human nature is fundamentally healthy and balanced. Except for diseases and defects from external sources, every child is born on the Fitrah (natural disposition). For this reason, creatures that are not endowed with reason are unsuitable for self-discipline. A wild animal that is cared for in its youth will not give up the hunt even as an adult.

Know that everyone has **three skills** and abilities:

THINKING ABILITY (REFLECTION AND CONTEMPLATION),

TALENT FOR DESIRE,

AND AN ABILITY TO BE ANGRY.

He whom ALLAH has honored with the gift of love for knowledge must perfect his ability to think. In doing so, ALLAH distinguishes him from animals and gives him a common point with the angels. This ability must outweigh the other two. This so that he becomes like the rider and his body like the horse. The rider dominates the horse because of his superiority. HE is indeed able to take him where he wants and end its life when he wishes.

Likewise, the intellectual faculty should dominate the other two faculties, using them at will. Only those who are successful deserve to be called "human".

Know that self-discipline is achieved through forbearance and transition from one level to another. It is achieved not by force but by forbearance.

It is then obtained by combining hope and fear. To strengthen it, it is advisable to keep good companions, move away from bad ones, study the Quran, think of the profitable stories of Paradise, of hell, and read the biographies of wise men and ascetics.

The pious predecessors allowed themselves to eat delicious food but some only granted themselves this reward after praying at night.

Sufyan Al-Thawri ate whatever he wanted.

Scholars and exegetes have always been lenient

with their souls and have remained so until they possess and subjugate them.

A neighbor of Malik ibn Dinar said:

One night I heard him talking to himself and saying:

"This is how you should be!"

The next morning I asked him:

"There was no one in your home, so who did you tell that?"

He replied, "My soul insisted on bread from me, so I withheld it for 3 days. Then I found a piece of dry bread. When I wanted to eat it, I said to myself, 'I'll have soft bread instead.' But my soul said to me, 'I'm happy with that (dry bread).'

So I replied, 'This is how you should be!'"

Know that when the soul knows that you are determined, it will also become determined. If it knows you are lazy, it will overwhelm you.

A poet said:

The rider knows how his horse works

So he keeps exhausting it by making it feel fearful.

One of the best practices for self-discipline is to keep track of every word, deed, neglect, and sin.

Even when self-discipline is achieved, the soul enjoys the exertions it endures.

Thabit Al-Banani said, "I endured the night [by praying in the night] for 20 years. Then I enjoyed the night (prayer) for (the next) 20 years. "

Abu Yazid said, "I insisted on turning my soul on my Lord while it cried until it finally smiled."

A poet said:

I laugh and cry every time I look

Until his eye was stained with my blood.

Yet we must not forget the rights of the soul. It's about rewarding it without compromising the goal of self-discipline. Indeed, if what it is generally trying to achieve is withheld from it, the heart will go blind, fear will spread, and the slave will feel constricted.

And know that for **ALLAH**, Exalted be **HE**, the value of the soul is greater than the value of worship. Therefore, he allowed the traveler to break the fast. However, only people with knowledge understand this.

CHAPTER 26: RAISING CHILDREN

The best education is that achieved at a young age. On the other hand, if the boy grows up with his character traits, it will be difficult to change him when he grows up.

A poet said:

If you straighten the branches, they adapt,

But the trunk won't go soft if you want to reform it.

Discipline gradually benefits the children

But it is of no use to those who have grown old.

Perseverance in discipline is an important principle, especially with children. In fact, it is beneficial in the sense that it becomes a habit for them.

A poet said:

Do not neglect the child's discipline,

Even if he complains of fatigue.

Note that the doctor will take into account the age, location, and time of the patient when prescribing medication. Likewise, discipline should be appropriate for each child, and signs of a child's success or failure can be seen at a very early age. The intelligent child is stimulated by learning, the less intelligent child is not.

A man once said to Sufyan Al-Thawri, "We beat our children if they don't pray." He replied, "You should rather encourage them and tell them the good news (if they are praying)."

Zubayd Al-Yafi used to say to little boys, "Whoever prays gets five walnuts."

Ibrahim ibn Adham said: "O my son! Study the science of the hadith. I will give you a dirham for every hadeeth you hear." Thanks to this, he began to study the hadeeth.

A father needs to know that his child is on deposit in his hands. He must therefore avoid him being in bad company from a young age. He must teach him good, because the child's heart is empty and collects everything that is put in it. He must make him love humility and generosity.

He has to dress him in white clothes. If he asks him for colored clothes, he must tell him that these are the clothes of women and females.

He must tell him the stories of the pious and make him avoid the love of poetry, for that is a seed that spoils. However, it should not prevent him from reading the poems about generosity and courage so that he may admire these qualities and become courageous.

His teacher should point out his mistakes and only reprimand him privately.

He must forbid him from overeating and sleeping. He has to get him used to eating what is sufficient and getting enough sleep, because that's better for his health.

The child needs to be physically active, such as walking. He should be forbidden to turn his back on people, to sneeze and yawn in their presence.

If he shows an attraction to a bad quality, it must be broken down very quickly before it becomes a habit. And when forbearance doesn't work, it's okay to discipline him.

Luqman said to his son:

"Oh my son! The discipline acts on the child like fertilizer when the seeds are sown."

If the little boy is aggressive, his father should be nice to him. Ibn 'Abbas said, "A young boy's aggressiveness is an improvement in his intelligence."

The wise men used to say, "Your son is like a flower for his first seven years, and your servant for the next seven years. When he turns fourteen and you've been good to him, he becomes your partner, and when you've been bad to him, he becomes your enemy."

A child should not be hit or insulted after they reach puberty. Otherwise, he will hope to lose his father in order to act as he wishes.

Anyone who turns 20 and has not turned virtuous is less likely to become an afterword, although they can. Hence, forbearance should be exercised with everyone.

Chapter 27: The Upbringing and Treatment of Wife

It is necessary to study this chapter in detail, for the most meritorious act is for a man to marry a virgin woman who knew no other before him.

The wise men said, "A virgin is with you and a non-virgin is against you." Moreover, it is a grave mistake to marry an older man to a young woman because she becomes such an enemy to him. This is because he cannot meet her needs and when her needs are not met she develops a natural aversion to him. So when a man married a young woman when he is old, he has to react to her dislike with mildness and spend a lot on her.

The man has to make himself beautiful for his wife, just as he would like her to make herself beautiful for him. he has to cover her body so that she can only see from him what he wants to see of her, and she has to do the same.

The husband shouldn't joke too often with his wife so that she doesn't put him down and become disobedient.

Also, he shouldn't put all of her money in her hands lest he be under her control as she could take all of his property and leave him.

ALLAH said:

"And do not entrust your goods to the weak, which **ALLAH** has made for your sustenance." (Al- Nisa 5)

Rather, he has to joke with her while maintaining his prestige and status.

The best way to raise a woman is to keep her from talking to other women (who are not virtuous or have bad personality traits) and to leave the house (unnecessarily).

She should also be assigned an elderly woman to raise her, teach her to show respect for her husband, and to educate her about the rights of men. She must behave as her protector, because the madness of youth is a dangerous thing.

If an older man marries a woman who is neither an immature young girl nor a woman weakened by old age, it is better for him because she is less arrogant and more respectful of him.

When a man is blessed with a woman who is exactly what he wants, he has to forget what he didn't get for the sake of what he has now. In fact, the branches are never mentioned when the roots are preserved. Also, there is a lot involved in having too many women, the least demanding of which is to look after them.

CHAPTER 28: UPBRINGING AND TREATMENT OF THE FAMILY

Know that when they see that you are above them in terms of your good or social status, your family members will envy you.

However, since it is forbidden to leave them, it is important to be smart about how to address them. It is appropriate to be kind to them without letting them know what they should not know.

One of the worst mistakes in dealing with family members is giving to some and depriving others. But if you want to do this anyway, you have to go to great lengths to hide it from them.

CHAPTER 29: LIFE IN SOCIETY

Everyone's nature is different. Therefore, it is difficult to get along with everyone. For this reason, solitude is the best choice because it brings great comfort and some relief.

However, when dealing with people is required, good behavior should be shown through forbearance and respect for their rights. For example, it is appropriate to ignore one's rights, be patient with the ignorant, forgive the unrighteous, and give the haughty the best place in meetings.

The two most effective ways to gain affection from others are forgiveness and generosity. Thanks to these two qualities, it becomes possible to turn the rebel into a loyal ally. It was mentioned in a hadith: "Treating people with wisdom is charity."

When the scholar is tested by the company of laypeople, he must be very careful. Indeed, the aims of the layperson are different from those of the scholar. What satisfies some, displeases others. Some of them hate the truth because they think it is wrong. So, despite their ignorance, they reject the words of the scholars.

Therefore the scholar has every interest in staying away from them. Their company will bring him only shame and humiliation in their eyes. They will then begin to discredit his knowledge.

In addition, when the fisherman sees a learned man laughing and eating, or hearing that he has married, the fisherman loses all respect for him [if, for example, he thinks he is in search of the joys of this lower world instead of the afterlife]. So you have to be very careful with these types of people because they are in fact the ones who killed the Prophets.

However, when a scholar is forced to hang out with them, be content with saying little and saying nothing that they could use against him. From there it will be possible to protect yourself from them.

Chapter 30: The Noble Character

The signs of a noble character are: righteousness and discipline with **ALLAH**'s permission, inclination to wisdom, determination in opinions and decisions, and an ever expanding mind, all from a young age.

ALLAH said:

"Indeed, We have put Ibrahim (Abraham) on the right path before." (Anbiya 51)

High characters are very often generous in their efforts and are saved from laziness. They enjoy being the leaders of other children during their childhood.

As they get older, good manners become their emblem without them even learning it.

Modesty and shyness are their adornment. Even the slightest knowledge and discipline affects them, as the grinding wheel affects steel, but not iron.

Then, when they reach the Age of Reason and discover the signs of their Creator's existence, when they understand what they were created for, when they meditate on the words addressed to them, their ultimate goal and the purpose of it all, they then start to work hard. This is because knowledge reveals the reality of things to them and they understand that whatever brings them closer to their Creator is better.

They then understand that the most effective way to get closer to Him is to learn the knowledge and act accordingly. Hence, they struggle to achieve all that their body can endure. Their intent awakens and their efforts multiply.

They realize that life is too short to contain all of knowledge, and they learn and keep only in each area they need as supplies for their quest.

They then work according to this knowledge and use their time because they fear that it will pass without them having achieved their goal.

They will therefore not waste a minute on what is unnecessary. They even use the time they spend eating and sleeping and remember the short time they were given.

As one poet put it:

Achieve your goals at full speed,

Because your age is nothing more than a journey among many others.

And gallop like horses and be the first

Because you borrowed them and you will return them at some point.

You always see such a person working to fill their time [with good deeds]. They conquer their passions in order to improve their situation.

They only learn useful knowledge because their hearts are preoccupied with setting goals over entertainment.

Their body is dedicated to **ALLAH** and His obedience. They are satisfied with what **ALLAH** has given them and do not ask people for anything. They forego other people's money and protect their honor. They then become better than them because they are independent and free themselves from their corruption by advising and admonishing one another.

When dealing with others, they act justly and fairly. They then rise above them in rank.

When asked for advice, they respond as best they can, but remain focused on their own reform while they are ready for their journey [from this world to the hereafter]. Their only concern is to prepare their luggage [their good works].

In this way, they save every second and strengthen themselves with a variety of provisions because they know that the way will be long. After all, they strive to structure their knowledge throughout their lives. As a result, their legacy is preserved even after their death.

They also ignore this world and only feed the amount that will allow them to reach the end of their day.

If they allow themselves more under the law than is necessary, their camel [soul] is strong enough to bear the burden.

So they remain under the grace of their Lord until what they accomplish gives them a deep love for him. Then they devote themselves to Him and indulge in His path so much that when people keep them company, only their body is with them, while their heart remains with their Creator all the time.

Such men are the favorites of **ALLAH** in His land. Those who seek the satisfaction of **ALLAH** want to breathe the same air as them. The scent of their truthfulness pours from their graves when they are buried.

When their works are mentioned, the seeker finds strength on his path to patience.

On the Day of Resurrection, the righteous who fear **ALLAH** will be like the star in the sky. It will look like the sun or the moon when it is full.

We ask **ALLAH** to give us the ability to imitate them, to give us their rank and noble character by His immense grace, because **HE** is the one who hears everything and is close to His servant.

May the prayers and peace of **ALLAH** be upon Muhammed, his family and his companions.